LET'S VISIT BOTSWANA

Let's visit
BOTSWANA

DENNIS E. GOULD

ACKNOWLEDGEMENTS

The Authors and Publishers are grateful to the following organizations and individuals for permission to reproduce copyright photographs in this book:

Botswana Development Corporation Limited; Botswana Meat Commission; Botswana National Archives; Camerapix Hutchison Library Limited; Alec Campbell; Buddy Dyck; John E. Gould; Brian Palmer; Elisabet da Rocha.

CIP data
Gould, Dennis E.
  Let's visit Botswana
  1. Botswana – Social life and customs – Juvenile Literature
  I. Title
  968.11'03   DT791

ISBN 0 222 01101 7

Burke Publishing Company Limited
Pegasus House, 116-120 Golden Lane, London EC1Y 0TL, England.
Burke Publishing (Canada) Limited
Registered Office: 20 Queen Street West, Suite 3000, Box 30, Toronto, Canada M5H 1V5.
Burke Publishing Company Inc.
Registered Office: 333 State Street, PO Box 1740, Bridgeport, Connecticut 06601, U.S.A.
Filmset in Baskerville by Graphiti (Hull) Ltd., Hull, England.
Printed in Singapore by Tien Wah Press (Pte.) Ltd.

Contents

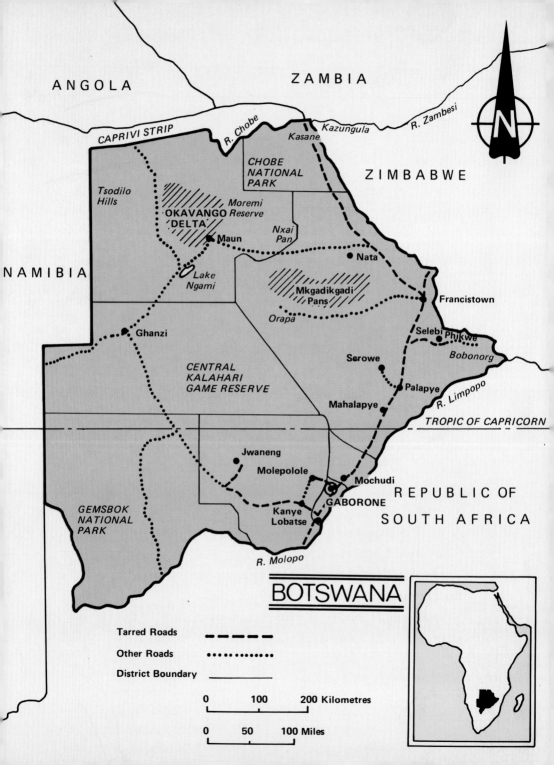

ANGOLA

ZAMBIA

CAPRIVI STRIP

R. Chobe

Kazungula

R. Zambesi

Kasane

CHOBE
NATIONAL
PARK

ZIMBABWE

Tsodilo
Hills

Moremi
Reserve

OKAVANGO
DELTA

Maun

Nxai
Pan

Nata

NAMIBIA

Lake
Ngami

Mkgadikgadi
Pans

Francistown

Orapa

Ghanzi

Selebi Phikwe

Bobonorg

Serowe

CENTRAL
KALAHARI
GAME RESERVE

Palapye

R. Limpopo

Mahalapye

TROPIC OF CAPRICORN

Jwaneng

Molepolole

Mochudi

REPUBLIC OF

GABORONE

Kanye
Lobatse

SOUTH AFRICA

GEMSBOK
NATIONAL
PARK

R. Molopo

BOTSWANA

Tarred Roads

Other Roads

District Boundary

| 0 | 100 | 200 Kilometres |

| 0 | 50 | 100 Miles |

A First Look at the Country

Botswana. Have you heard of this country before? There are many people who have not. If you have heard of it, do you think you know in which continent it is situated? It is in Africa. But Africa is a huge continent with many countries and dozens of them have changed their names in recent decades. Can you get any closer in placing the position of Botswana?

It is in southern Africa. If you look at the map, you will see that it is land-locked. That means that it has no coast-line and is completely surrounded by other countries. In fact, it is more than five hundred kilometres (over three hundred miles) to the sea in any direction.

Botswana's neighbours are Zimbabwe, South Africa and South West Africa (which has been struggling for many years to be recognized as an independent country, called Namibia). Another neighbouring country is Zambia, but the border with that nation is very unusual. To the north of Botswana is the River Zambesi. The boundaries of four countries meet at one point in the middle of that river, and Zambia is one of them.

Much of Botswana is bordered by rivers, giving the country an irregular shape as they meander; but to the west, the borders with Namibia do not follow natural landmarks; they are straight lines following man-made boundaries. In the north-west is the

Caprivi Strip, a wedge of land which separates Angola and Zambia from Botswana. The Caprivi Strip is part of Namibia, another of the countries which meet in the River Zambesi, together with Zimbabwe and Botswana.

Most people who visit Botswana, from any great distance away, fly there. As the country is land-locked, it cannot be reached by sea without a very long and slow journey overland for the last part of the trip. It is most usual to fly to one of the large international airports in neighbouring countries, such as Johannesburg in South Africa, Harare in Zimbabwe or Lusaka, the capital of Zambia. From those places local flights continue the journey to Botswana. But now, as from 1985, a new airport

A view of the Chobe River, which forms the natural border between northern Botswana and the Caprivi Strip of Namibia

should be ready to receive major international flights directly into Gaborone, Botswana's capital.

The whole of Botswana is in the southern hemisphere and the northern half of the country is in the tropics; it lies north of the Tropic of Capricorn—the imaginary line of latitude which is 23° 30' south of the Equator. This is the most southerly latitude where the sun is directly overhead at noon. This happens on December 21st, the longest day of the year in this hemisphere. But the length of the day varies very little within these latitudes of Botswana. The day is usually approximately 6.00 a.m. to 6.00 p.m. and, depending on the season, alters by no more than an hour from those times, either earlier or later.

It is strange, for someone who has not been to the tropics before, to see the rays of sunlight streaming straight down the chimney onto the fireplace, at midday. Out-of-doors, shadows disappear almost completely when the sun is overhead.

Although Botswana is fairly close to the Equator and could be expected to have a hot climate, the temperature is somewhat lowered because most of the country is situated on the Southern Central African Plateau—a table of flat land which is about 1,000 metres (over 3,000 feet) above sea-level.

However, it does get warm during the summer months— between September and April. Then the temperature is usually around 25 degrees Centigrade (about 75 degrees Fahrenheit) during the daytime. This is very pleasant, especially as the air is not humid. But during the months of November to February the temperature climbs to between 30 degrees and 35 degrees

9

A typical arid landscape with stunted trees and bushes

Centigrade (86 and 95 degrees Fahrenheit), and sometimes even up to 40 degrees Centigrade (105 degrees Fahrenheit) in the shade. And then the temperatures do not drop so much at night.

During the winter months of May, June and July it becomes very cool after dusk and even frost is not uncommon during the night. However, the temperature seldom sinks many degrees below freezing-point. And by about nine o'clock in the morning, the sun is usually shining warmly again.

Botswana is a very arid country. More than four-fifths of the land is classified as desert, although this must not be confused with the kinds of desert which are seen in pictures of the sand-dunes of the Sahara. It is more often bare, waste stretches of very dry soil, dotted with stunted trees and bushes. In areas where trees are able to survive more readily, the most common are the mophane and various kinds of acacia. Their leaves are specially adapted to the hard climate of summer.

In some parts of the country there is very little rainfall. But in other parts, which are still quite arid, the amount of rainfall averages about 475 millimetres (just under 20 inches) a year. One reason for the dry ground is that the rain falls in very concentrated periods of time and runs off the surface without soaking in, or else disappears into the sandy soil. Another problem is that the heat causes a great loss of moisture from the land, by evaporation. The rain falls, moisture rises as water vapour during the heat of the day, gathers in storm-clouds during the late afternoon and then falls again in another heavy downpour. And there are often quite violent thunderstorms.

Drought can be a very serious problem in Botswana and the

Watering cattle. Lack of water is a serious problem, and drought often brings great hardship to the people and their animals

surrounding areas of southern Africa. If there are two or three successive years of limited rainfall, life becomes very difficult for the people and the cattle on which so many of them depend for their livelihood. In recent decades, these periods of drought have been recurring about every ten or twelve years, and they last for two or three years.

Botswana is not a very large country by African standards; it is about the size of France, being just under 600,000 square kilometres (310,000 square miles) in area. But, in spite of remarkable increases in population, in recent years, the number of inhabitants is less than one million. According to the 1983 census, the population was 936,600. This showed a tremendous increase of more than sixty per cent since 1971. But Botswana is still one of the least densely populated countries in the world.

The People

One way in which Botswana differs from many other African countries is that it is not really troubled by tribalism. This is partly due to the historical development of the country. The people have a deep-rooted sense of belonging to one nation, in addition to their allegiance to a particular chief. In more recent years it has been a conscious policy of the leaders of Botswana to weld the people into one unit with loyalty to their country, and thus avoid the damage caused by the tribalism which has been seen in so many other African countries. All too often, Africans have gained independence from colonial domination only to revive long-standing quarrels and rivalries between different tribes.

Botswana is helped in this respect by the fact that the people have no difficulty in communicating with each other. Almost all Batswana (as the people are called) speak to each other in Setswana (except the Bushmen) and for the vast majority this is their natural language. In fact, however, the official language of Botswana is English, although this is seldom used in everyday conversation by a Motswana.

The words Botswana, Batswana, Setswana and Motswana have a common element—Tswana—which is the name of the ethnic group from which the majority of the population of

Botswana originate. They came to this area in the seventeenth century, but about seventy-five per cent of the Tswana are spread throughout parts of southern Africa. The word Botswana means "the land of the Tswana". The previous name of this country, Bechuanaland, was an attempt to capture the sound of the name of the country, as pronounced by its inhabitants, and to express it in English spelling.

A Motswana is an individual person of the Tswana nation. Batswana is the plural (several Motswana) or it may even refer to the whole people. Setswana is their language.

Although Botswana is in the happy position of being relatively free from tribal disputes, this does not mean that there are not sub-divisions and linguistic differences among the population. There are, in fact, eight main tribes in Botswana. There are also some smaller groups of different origin. These include the so-called Bushmen, the Basarwa, who are the original inhabitants of southern Africa; the Mbukushu who fled from Angola early in the nineteenth century; and the Herero who settled in the north-west of Botswana. Many Herero fled into the country from neighbouring Namibia, after a war with the Germans at the beginning of this century. Their womenfolk are easily distinguished by their dress. In the north-east, in particular, there are many Kalanga. About a quarter of that tribe live in this part of Botswana, whereas the remainder live across the border in Matabeleland, Zimbabwe. It is the Kalanga who represent the main signs of tribalism in Botswana. For example, they have pressed for schools in Botswana with

A Herero woman. When the first German missionaries and their wives arrived in southern Africa in the late nineteenth century, they were horrified to find that the Herero wore virtually no clothing. Eventually the women were persuaded to dress as the missionaries' wives did—and they have worn the same style ever since!

their language as the official language of the classroom.

During the time when Bechuanaland was a British protectorate, the eight main tribes were each given a region, with a capital village. The members of one tribe could not live or work in the region of another, without permission from the chief of that region.

The Bamangwato are the dominant tribe. It is the Bamangwato who have produced the country's past great leaders. The first President of Botswana, Sir Seretse Khama, was a member of that tribe. So too was his grandfather who, as Khama III, was known as Khama the Great. The members

15

of the Bamangwato make up about forty per cent of the population and their lands cover more than one-fifth of the area of Botswana. The main historical events in Botswana in the last two centuries are linked to the leaders of the Bamangwato. Their tribal capital is in Serowe, the largest traditional village in Botswana, and probably in Africa, with a population of between 30,000 and 40,000.

The Bakwena regard themselves as being the oldest tribe in Botswana. The Bamangwato broke away from them, before white men appeared in the area. Molepolole is their capital. It

A Bamangwato mother and her children outside their mud hut

was with this tribe that the well-known missionary-explorer, David Livingstone, first settled.

The Bangwaketse, along with the Bamangwato and Bakwena, formed three branches into which the Tswana ethnic group divided. The tribal capital of the Bangwaketse is situated in Kanye, in the south-east corner of Botswana.

Availability of water is the main factor which determines the pattern of human settlement. About eighty per cent of the people in Botswana live in the eastern part of the country, which is the catchment area of the Limpopo River, where the soil is fairly fertile and there is sufficient rainfall to support arable farming and cattle-rearing. Thus, seven of the eight main tribes live on the eastern side of the country,

The Batawana is the eighth tribe, and these people are to be found in the north-west, in the region known as Ngamiland. Within this region is the famous Okavango Delta. The capital of the Batawana is Maun. Two non-Tswana tribes also live in this region, the Herero and the Mbukushu; the latter living mainly in the swamps.

The remaining major tribes live on the south-east border and have only small areas of tribal land. One of them, the Bakgatla, fled from the Transvaal (South Africa), being driven out by the Dutch settler farmers, known as Boers. The capital of their area of settlement is Mochudi. There are still many of the tribe living in South Africa, but they recognize Chief Pilane, in Botswana, as their chief.

Unlike many of the tribes which take their name from that

The main factor in determining where people live in Botswana is the availability of water. This picture shows drilling for water

of a person, the Batlokwa are the "people of Tlokwe", a town in the Transvaal. In 1880, a chief named Gaberone left the main tribe and took his followers to settle in land belonging to the Bakwena. However, when Chief Gaberone died, the place was renamed after him. Some thirty odd years later, in 1966, it became the site of an entirely new capital of the newly-founded Republic of Botswana, though it is now written as Gaborone. The Batlokwa tribe is the smallest in numbers.

The Bamalete live in the north-east and are not of Tswana origin. They came from the Nguni tribe in the Transvaal, in

1852. Their capital is Ramotswa. They have been completely absorbed into the customs and language of the Tswana.

The remaining major tribe, the Baralong, are only a small part of the large tribe in South Africa. Their capital is Mafeking, in a part of South Africa now called Bophutatswana. Before Gaborone became the new capital of Botswana, the capital of Bechuanaland had actually been Mafeking, then in South Africa. It is very seldom indeed that a country has had its capital outside its own borders.

Two other small groups, originally from central Africa, have settled in the north, near the Chobe River. They are the Yei and the Subiya. Another two small groups, who live in the Kalahari Desert area, are the Bakgalagadi and the Lala. Kgalagadi means "great thirst land". Both groups are mixed peoples related to the Bushmen.

With such a mixture of peoples it is admirable that they live together in reasonable peace.

In addition to the tribes, there are two completely different peoples: Europeans and Asians. They include several different nationalities. Botswana has only about 12,000 non-Africans and of these only about 5,000 are permanent residents. Since having control of her own affairs, Botswana has restricted the flow of foreigners into the country.

Many of the white temporary population are in Botswana in connection with some form of aid programme. But the government's policy is quite clearly that of "localization". This means that the Batswana are being trained to take over and run things themselves, without the need of expatriate guidance.

When considering the relatively peaceful relations in Botswana, compared with most other African countries, the smooth transition to Independence and the continuing development since, it is perhaps appropriate to remember two factors which distinguish Botswana from other African countries. Botswana was not conquered, or colonized, in the first place. Secondly, Independence was not accompanied by bloodshed; it was a peaceful agreed handing-over of sovereignty.

The Country in Past Years

The story of the peoples of Botswana has been passed down from generation to generation by word of mouth. It was not until European missionaries entered the region that written records were kept. It was Robert Moffat, of the London Missionary Society, who first settled amongst the Tswana in 1820. He founded a village at Kuruman. (A later northwards shift of the border has resulted in Kuruman now being in South Africa.) Journals kept by Moffat, and by later missionaries, give us a more reliable means of piecing together events in the nineteenth century.

However, there is evidence from long before that time that there were settled groups of people in Botswana even in the fourth century. And before that the land was thinly populated by wandering bands of Bushmen (Basarwa) who lived by hunting and gathering food.

The forefathers of the members of Botswana's present-day dominant tribes were led by a chief called Masilo. He lived in the middle of the seventeenth century. It was his three grandsons, Kwena, Ngwato and Ngwaketse who gave their names to the three leading tribes; the Bakwena, Bamangwato and Bangwaketse.

In the beginning of the nineteenth century, the region was

Robert Moffat, of the London Missionary Society, who settled among the Tswana people in 1820

invaded and attacked by the Matabele. All the chiefs were defeated, with the exception of Sekgoma, who was the leader of the Bamangwato. The latter succeeded in driving off the Matabele, who were then further defeated by the Boers.

It was the Boers' search for new farming lands and then the discovery of gold and other minerals that were the reasons behind the unrest and strife in the eastern area of the country at these times. The Matabele withdrew to the region north of the River Limpopo, which is in the country today called Zimbabwe.

In 1841, another missionary came on the scene in this area of strife between Matabele, Batswana and Boers. He was David Livingstone, a qualified doctor of medicine and trained scientist. He became world-famous and is, probably, better known for his journeys of discovery than as a missionary. He was the first white man to see the gigantic waterfalls which he named Victoria Falls.

David Livingstone lived in Bechuanaland for more than ten years. He settled amongst the Bakwena, whose chief was Sechele. Livingstone succeeded in converting Chief Sechele to Christianity and he gave his support to the Bakwena in their struggles against the Boers in the Transvaal. The Bakwena were happy in their established beliefs that animals, trees and even inanimate objects had spirits which must be treated with reverence. Such a religion is known as animism.

Livingstone decided to move northwards to find other peoples to help with medicine and conversion. Soon after his

David Livingstone, the famous scientist and explorer. He was the first white man to see the gigantic waterfalls which he named the Victoria Falls, in honour of Queen Victoria

departure, gold was discovered in the region of Bechuanaland which was called Tati—after a river of that name.

This was the first discovery of gold in southern Africa by white men. It was at Monarch Mine. The remains of the derelict mine are close to present-day Francistown ("the capital of the North") and they are easily visited. A short scramble up the slopes is rewarded by a fine view over the town and the surrounding settlements.

The Boers moved northwards to drive out the Bamangwato who inhabited the region, and they claimed the Tati area. Missionaries strongly recommended the British government to assist the Batswana, but their requests were turned down.

But a leader was to come from amongst the Batswana themselves. The outstanding personality in the history of the Batswana is the son of Sekgoma, Khama III. He became Chief of the Bamangwato in 1872 and has been called Khama the Great. He built up a small but well-trained band of fighters which deterred the Matabele from renewing their attacks. Khama III co-operated with the missionaries in his country and was converted to Christianity and baptized in 1860. He supported mission schools and introduced the total abolition of alcoholic drink.

Khama III was a clever diplomat. He wanted to unify the peoples of all the tribes so as not to allow the Europeans to dominate his country, as had been the case in many parts of Africa. Yet, at the same time, he needed assistance to fight against the Boers. He turned to the British for help, but wanted a promise that the chiefs would continue to hold full power in Bechuanaland (as Botswana then was).

The British drew up an agreement with the Boers that they were not to cross the River Limpopo, but the raids continued and little was done by the British to make certain that the agreement was respected.

Meanwhile, many Germans had emigrated to the area now known as Namibia. The British became anxious about being squeezed between the Germans to the west and the Boers to the east. The British sent an armed force—after repeated attempts to get the Boers to recognize the border had been ignored. Khama and the other chiefs welcomed this aid.

In 1885, the area to the south of present-day Botswana became part of the Cape Colony and was called British Bechuanaland. Nowadays, the region belongs to South Africa. The land north of the Molopo River, as far as latitude 22° South, became the Bechuanaland Protectorate. It was not until 1891 that the boundary was moved further north to become the same as that of present-day Botswana.

At this time, the British Empire was at the height of its power. Queen Victoria's realm extended over much of the world. Consequently, this insignificant, land-locked country, with no known minerals of value and only a small number of British subjects to protect, seemed to be unworthy of much attention or expense. The only real interest was in keeping open the line of communication linking the Cape Colony with present day Zimbabwe and its rich mines.

Monarch Gold Mine, the first site at which white men discovered gold in southern Africa. Attempts have recently been made to mine here again

It is therefore not surprising that the British were prepared to allow Cecil Rhodes, and his British South Africa Company, to take over the administration of the area, at a rent of £4,000 per annum.

Rhodes, and his company, already dominated the area known as Zimbabwe (previously called Rhodesia after Cecil Rhodes). Rhodes dreamed of British domination of Africa, from Cape Town to Cairo, with a railway link from north to south.

Khama III and the other chiefs were very frightened of the outcome of this proposal and were shocked that their "protectors" would even consider handing over their land to those who would certainly exploit the native inhabitants. They were also afraid of the effect of the introduction of alcohol, which they felt sure would accompany such an invasion.

Together with two other leading chiefs, Khama III travelled to London, in 1895, to plead with Queen Victoria. They were accompanied by a Reverend Willoughby, who went to help them with their appeals. The outcome was a compromise. The country was to remain a British protectorate, with the chiefs still holding power as before. But, in exchange, they had to relinquish land on which Rhodes would build his railway.

Just a month after their return to Africa there was a significant change in events. The administrator of Rhodes' company led a private army from the protectorate to support an uprising in Johannesburg. This—the Jameson Raid—was a failure. As a result, Rhodes became the scapegoat and fell out of favour with the British government, who took away his rights in the protectorate.

The protectorate was, therefore, administered by the British for the next seventy years, from Mafeking, south of the Molopo River.

Eventually, war broke out between the British and the Boers. There was fighting between 1899 and 1902. After final victory, the British decided to create a Union of South Africa to include all their possessions within the area. The chiefs of Bechuanaland, however, did not wish to be included in this Union. They feared that they would lose control of their land and their rights. They

Khama III *(seated right)* and two other Batswana chiefs, with the Reverend W. C. Willoughby. These four men travelled to London in 1895 to petition against their land being handed over to Cecil Rhodes and the British South Africa Company

were not forced to join when the Union was formed in 1910, but it was made clear that they would have to become part of the Union of South Africa at some stage in the future.

Britain did little to help develop Bechuanaland—an unproductive region which they expected to pass to the Union very soon. There followed a period when the British made occasional gestures to show their official authority, but in the main, the chiefs were allowed to rule.

Towards Independence

Then the British began to think that the chiefs had too much power over their people. As a result, a Native Advisory Council was formed in 1920. It was the first organized form of co-operation between the colonial authorities and the local representatives of the tribes.

In the 1930s the influence of the British increased and they attempted to reduce the power of the chiefs. They also tried to curtail the traditional system of local law courts, called the *kgotla*. Resistance to these measures was led by another great member of the Bamangwato tribe and Khama family, Tshekedi Khama. When Khama III had died in 1923, he was succeeded by his son. However, this son also died, just two years later. The chieftainship passed to the grandson of Khama III, Seretse Khama. But Seretse was only four years old. Consequently, a regent temporarily took over the rule, in place of the young chief. This was Tshekedi Khama, Seretse's uncle, and the youngest son of Khama III.

Tshekedi worked slowly and steadily towards a situation where the native people of Bechuanaland had more control over their own lives and affairs. Unity amongst the tribes was further strengthened and a sense of national identity was intensified.

When the Second World War broke out, in 1939, some ten

thousand men from the tribes of Bechuanaland went to serve on the side of the Allies, being encouraged so to do by the chiefs. Those who returned from the war did so with a much greater awareness of the outside world. This fact, together with the increasing racial discrimination in the Union of South Africa, led to an ever-growing desire for independence. The Batswana were ever fearful of being forced into that Union.

However, in spite of repeated requests and demands by the Union for Bechuanaland to be incorporated, the British had taken the stand that they would only agree to this if the Batswana chose it themselves. With the Union's policy of *apartheid* (separate development), which forces the great number of Blacks to be separated from the small number of ruling Whites, and which gives the Blacks no voting rights, there was little likelihood that the Batswana would elect to join.

When, soon after the end of the Second World War, Seretse Khama came of age and could have taken over the chieftainship from his uncle, he asked to be allowed to go to England first, in order to study for a law degree at Oxford University. Tshekedi continued as regent and Seretse went to Oxford, where he met Ruth Williams. In 1948 they were married.

This event caused international reactions. The Whites in Southern Africa thought that it would undermine their policies against inter-racial marriage. Tshekedi also objected to the marriage; and many of the Bamangwato felt that Seretse no longer had the right to be their chief since he had married a white woman. They argued that he should have sought permission to marry, as was tribal tradition. They also complained that future heirs would not be pure Bamangwato, but of mixed race. But opinions wavered. At the *kgotla* meeting, it was decided that Seretse should not be accepted as chief. Later, the decision was reversed. Then the British government acted, prompted by South Africa. Seretse was banished from his home and country, where he was chief-elect, and he was exiled in London. Tshekedi, too, was made to leave his tribal region. He lived in exile with the Bakwena, where he still continued his efforts towards eventual independence.

Repeated requests from South Africa for Bechuanaland to be forced into the Union gave Tshekedi the opening to argue that his people had no representation and could not, therefore, speak officially on behalf of their country. Tshekedi was allowed to return to his home, but not in any official capacity.

In 1956, Tshekedi met Seretse in London and persuaded him to give up his claim to the chieftainship of the Bamangwato. After Seretse had agreed to this, the British terminated his exile. The two men returned to their homeland as ordinary members of the tribe.

When Tshekedi died, in 1959, he could not have imagined that, by sacrificing the chieftainship, Seretse would attain an even higher position in the land. Nor did Tshekedi live to see the formation of the Legislative Council in 1960, although in many ways it was the fruit of his early labours.

The stage was now set for Bechuanaland to have a government of its own. By this time, many other nations in

Africa had gained independence. Awareness of this possibility began to spread amongst the people. But, at this time, there were no political parties in the country. The first party was formed in December 1960. It was called the Bechuanaland People's Party. This party was impatient for Black power and wanted to rid the country of the Whites. Seretse Khama began to interest himself actively in politics. He could not agree with the nationalistic and racist policy of the B.P.P. and he formed another party—the Bechuanaland Democratic Party. He urged integration, realizing that ''one man, one vote'' would create no great political influence if limited to the small White minority.

The sudden upsurge of interest in independence seemed to come as a surprise to the British authorities. They considered that the poorly developed country was not really ready to take on the responsibilities that go with freedom. But they had to go along with the demands.

In 1963, the position was reviewed and a plan for internal self-rule was proposed. Preparations were made for national elections, which revealed a considerably larger population than had been estimated. In 1964, there were just over half a million inhabitants of what is now Botswana.

The country was divided into thirty-one constituencies, and voters were registered. Symbols representing the parties (to overcome the problems of illiteracy) were established. A most important move was the building of an entirely new capital. Obviously, a new, independent country could not continue to have its capital outside its borders. This new capital was sited at Gaborone. In just a few years, a capital was erected where there had previously been only "bush". It is situated in the south-east corner of the country, and is served by the railway.

Seeing the direction in which the country was now inevitably heading, many people, predictably, were critical. Nevertheless, the more general reaction was eager anticipation of independence. Some elements of the White population made desperate efforts to prevent integration and the anticipated loss of power and privilege. Some of the chiefs, too, were afraid that their role would be diminished. Some were disappointed that Seretse Khama was not more outspoken in his denouncement of South Africa's policy of *apartheid* and that he did not propose more definite action.

On March 1st, 1965, seventy-five per cent of the registered voters went to the polls. The calmer approach of Seretse Khama and the realistic acceptance of the country's problems, which the Democratic Party had adopted, resulted in twenty-eight of the thirty-one constituencies choosing the symbol of the automobile jack, which represented the Democratic Party of Seretse Khama.

Thus, Seretse Khama was officially asked by the British representatives in the country to become prime minister. He entered the new legislative assembly knowing that his party had received about eighty-five per cent of the votes cast.

Seretse made known that full independence was only a year and a half away, and that Bechuanaland would first be known as Botswana Protectorate and, after Independence Day, as the

Sir Seretse Khama reading the new constitution on Independence Day, 1st October, 1966

Republic of Botswana. It would continue to be a member of the British Commonwealth, as the Commonwealth of Nations was still then called.

In spite of his triumph, Seretse had a difficult task ahead of him. Bechuanaland was amongst the twenty-five poorest nations in the world. He had to "walk a tightrope" diplomatically, and his country was suffering a very severe drought. At that time, cattle-rearing was the only real industry in the country, and one out of every three beasts did not survive these terrible five years of water shortage. The threatened famine was only averted by outside aid. Such conditions did not seem very promising for a proud little country that wanted to be independent.

On September 30th, 1966, the Republic of Botswana gained full independence. The forty-five year old returned exile, the deposed tribal chief, was now Sir Seretse Khama, first President of Botswana.

Agriculture

Botswana is still slowly overcoming the difficulties in its struggle following independence. But being independent did not remove the recurring struggle against drought. Foot-and-mouth disease was an ever-present threat in this country which depended so heavily on its cattle as the main source of income.

However, Botswana did have one great stroke of good fortune. In 1967 the first diamond pipe (of worthwhile value) was

Donkeys pulling a plough—quite a common sight. About eighty per cent of households are directly involved in agriculture

discovered at Orapa. This was the second largest pipe known to exist in the world. Others were found later. Prospecting had been going on for a dozen years before this success. But, before we examine the mining of diamonds and other minerals, let us take a look at the industry which is still referred to as "the backbone of the nation", namely agriculture.

Agriculture directly involves about eighty per cent of the households in the country. The nation's plans for development pay great attention to the improvement of traditional farming methods, in order to help small farmers produce more and make their yields more dependable.

A change of policy over recent decades has removed the chief's domination over the land and the cattle. Individuals now feel a greater personal interest in the fruits of their labours. Botswana is not self-sufficient, and farmers are being encouraged to look upon food crops as a source of extra income and to aim at producing more than just what they need for themselves. A central Marketing Board provides a guaranteed market at fixed prices. But it is difficult to persuade farmers to change from the generations-old tradition of cattle-rearing to another form of agriculture more suited to their local conditions to modern aids and methods.

The main subsistence crops are sorghum and maize. These are usually grown for more or less immediate use. Women pounding the "mealie" grain in hollowed-out wooden containers, using long, heavy poles, are a very common sight in Botswana. Mealie porridge forms the staple diet. Sorghum

Two women pounding maize in a hollowed wooden container. Mealie porridge forms the staple diet for most Batswana

stands up to the arid climate better than maize. It is grown over a large area of the country and is used for food in many forms. Sorghum is also used in the brewing of local beer.

Experiments to grow cotton in irrigated areas have met with success and there are hopes of this increasing. Other experiments include growing rice in the damp Okavango Delta region.

Citrus trees grow in Botswana, and potatoes (often the so-called "sweet potatoes") and other vegetables are cultivated. But it is a real struggle for smallholdings to produce a reliable yield. Netting is used to provide shade but this can only be afforded on a small scale. Amongst the more successful crops

An aerial view of rice-fields in the Okavango Delta

are peas and beans, sunflowers (grown for the oil from the seeds), millet, groundnuts, melons and squash (similar to pumpkin).

The Batswana have kept and raised cattle for generations. Traditionally, most of the cattle were tribally owned—and controlled, on behalf of the tribe, by the chief. They were part of the tribal structure and no important festivity took place without the involvement of cattle, in some way. (Sometimes they were ceremonially slaughtered.)

Although many Batswana today are owners of a small number of cattle or work with them, the bulk of the national herd—three million head—is still owned by only a small percentage of the population. The cattle have a difficult time in periods of drought; sometimes hundreds of thousands die or have to

38

be slaughtered. However, the climate basically favours open cattle-grazing. There are some lush grasslands in the north, but the majority of cattle are on large ranches in the central and southern districts. Mixtures of breeds have produced animals which can better endure the dry conditions. The Brahman cow, easily identified by the hump on its shoulders, can do well in Botswana. It grows more quickly than the local, tougher Tswana beast, which can go for up to three days without water.

Experience has been gained over hundreds of years and this has now contributed towards Botswana having one of the largest and most sophisticated meat industries in Africa. The Botswana Meat Commission was established in 1966, the year of

Cattle and goats at a waterhole. The lack of water is a serious problem in Botswana; many animals may die in periods of drought

Independence. It created one of the largest processing plants in Africa, situated in Lobatse, in the far south-east. The plant is a modern, well-organized, integrated complex of abattoir, cannery, tannery, producer of by-products and research centre. It has been virtually the only abattoir in the country, but a new one is being established in the north, at Maun. This will avoid the necessity for transporting cattle long distances by rail or by huge road vehicles. The BMC is responsible for all exports of beef from Botswana. Because of the BMC's high standards, the meat is accepted into world-wide markets. In addition, visitors to Botswana are able to enjoy eating beefsteaks at a low price.

One of the great problems with cattle in Botswana is that of over grazing. This is made worse by an almost unashamed policy of quantity in preference to quality. Even numerous boreholes for water tend to result in cattle congregating and overgrazing an area. To a Motswana, a cow is like money in the bank—to be sold when some extra expense arises.

The main problem in milk production is the unreliable water supply. The water supply must be regular throughout the year for dairy cattle to do well. In Selebi-Phikwe, an experiment with irrigation shows signs of promise. Apart from anything else, it saves the country spending money on foreign exchange for milk imports. Otherwise, dairy farming is very limited; each farmer keeps perhaps just a cow or two to supply his own immediate needs. Goats are an additional source of milk in rural communities. They also provide meat. About seventy-five per cent of rural households keep small herds of goats, as these stand

Men working in the de-boning room of the Botswana Meat Commission's packing section in Lobatse. This is one of Africa's most modern meat-processing plants

up to the drought better than cows. Sheep are far less often seen, although in the remote south-western region Karakul sheep are bred for their valuable curly pelts.

There is plenty of water in the Okavango Delta area, but there are also plenty of tse-tse flies which can be fatal to man and beast. Spraying with insecticide is helping to eradicate the problem.

With the ever-increasing growth of urban areas in Botswana, the demand for eggs and poultry to be supplied to the towns has created a need for these items to be produced commercially. This is just one of several new branches of agriculture. The aim is to achieve self-reliance and to avoid the need to import.

How the Batswana Live......and Play

The people of Botswana differ from most other African peoples in the arrangement of their homes. They usually have houses in two or three places, sometimes far apart.

There is the cattle-post, where the "home" is not usually a permanent building. It is called the *mogwaafatshe*, meaning "get down on hands and knees". To make it, several poles are placed in a circle and tied at the top to form a cone. Small branches are woven between the poles and long grasses are tied in place. A thornbush fence surrounds the structure.

The cattle-post is the man's domain. It is the only place where he will cook and do jobs which have been traditionally regarded as women's work. Young boys look after the herds and keep them together, as the cattle are not usually in fenced areas. In the past this meant that there was a tendency for girls to be allowed to attend school more than boys. Now that school attendance is free, however, education is more eagerly sought. In addition, the policy of tribal lands is changing so that more areas are fenced, and the tradition of herd-boys is also slowly changing.

A second home is traditionally at the "lands". This is often better kept than the village home, because the families leave their villages as soon as the first rains come and may remain

42

at the "lands" until they have harvested the crops. Development is now altering social patterns. Improved roads make travel between village and lands a lot easier. Schooling results in children staying in the village during the week, to join their mother, brothers and sisters at the weekend. It is usually the girls who work on the lands.

Some aspects of development also bring about social problems. There is usually a "generation gap" in most countries; parents and teenage children have different opinions. But in rapidly-changing Botswana this gap is even wider, especially as, traditionally, there has always been such respect for age and experience.

The village home is probably in a very large community.

Typical village houses, consisting of clay and dung walls, with poles outside the building to support the grass-thatched roof

Building the *lolwapa* (courtyard) walls outside a typical village house. The walls are carefully daubed with a mixture of mud and cow-dung which dries hard in the sun

Botswana's villages are unusual in this respect. People return to their home village during the winter. The traditional home, called *ntlo yo bojang* (meaning "house of grass"), is still the one most commonly seen in the country. It is constructed by using clay and dung walls on a circular stone foundation. The roof is not connected to the walls but a ring of poles support it from the outside. These vertical poles are held firmly in place by a clay seat which surrounds the house. Green branches are lashed to the top of the poles in a horizontal ring. Through these a cone of poles is interlaced by more green branches and thatch.

44

This type of home is cool in summer because a breeze can enter between the walls and roof. But it is not so comfortable during the winter. A small fire may be lit inside.

A more modern type of house is called the *rantafole*, taken from the Afrikaans name for this kind of round house, *rondavel*. In these houses, the foundation and walls are usually a combination of clay and cement. The walls are made with bricks, perhaps still made of sun-baked clay. The houses have a wooden door, and probably one window. The thatching is carefully done to make the structure more watertight for when the rains come. Sometimes a metal cone is placed over the top to make it even more watertight. Some of these modern *rantafoles* are quite spacious and are even divided into rooms. The growing tendency to sleep on beds rather than on the floor has meant that square houses are now being built, basically in the same manner, since they are more suitable for modern furniture.

The basic unit of the village is the *kgotla*. All the relatives of the father group themselves into a *kgotla*. Usually it consists of a number of families that all have the same father or grandfather, together with one or two families who have joined them. The *kgotla* (ward) is the home, and the *lolwapa* (courtyard) of each family helps to form a large circle around the central cattle kraal (enclosure). Each *kgotla* has its own headman. The village is a collection of such *kgotla*, and all of them are presided over by one chief. A really large village—such as Serowe, Kanye or Molepolole—may consist of more than a hundred such wards, with a total population of between 30,000 and 40,000.

A *rondavel,* a rather more modern form of housing. A metal cone has been placed over the top of the thatching to make the roof more watertight

In the *kgotla*, local matters are discussed and minor justice administered. Flogging is still not uncommon.

Another social link is the totem. Traditionally, in Botswana, if an animal was somehow connected with the people it became their symbol (totem) and they believed it would bring them bad luck if a member of the community killed it. If a Motswana praises the same animal as another man, even though he is a stranger, there is a sense of comradeship between them. Crocodiles, monkeys, baboons and duikers (small antelope) are some of the main totems. Even though most young people still know to which totem they owe allegiance, it is a tradition which is fast disappearing with the increase of westernization.

With the increased movement towards living in towns, growing numbers of Batswana are living in more modern brick buildings, of low, medium, or high cost. The low-cost structures are very simple and rather crude in appearance. The huge outside toilet often seems not to be very much smaller than the house. On the other hand, a newly built development of medium- and high-cost bungalows and houses in Francistown looks as though it had been transported from a housing site in England.

A *kgotla* meeting discussing local matters in the village of Molepolole. The *kgotla* is usually made up of a number of related families, and there may be many *kgotla* in a large town or village

This game, called *mmila,* is very popular in Botswana. It is played with stones on a "board" marked out in the sand

It has been said that the living standard of a country can be quickly assessed by studying the toy-shops. Well, until very recent years there were no toy-shops in Botswana. Children had no manufactured toys. But, in the towns nowadays, there is evidence of the truth of this comment. Some quite sophisticated toys are appearing, as well as plenty of poor quality rubbish. In the villages, the skipping-rope and the ball are about all that there is in the way of playthings. And the "ball" may be knotted rags or an empty tin can. One novel "toy" to be seen very often is a model car, made out of bits of wire. Often it is ingeniously arranged so that it can be steered as it is pushed.

Schools in Botswana have introduced sports, and football is very popular throughout the country. The Batswana did not inherit cricket from the British, but they do enjoy another game called soft-ball, which is something like baseball. An interest in tennis is also slowly being fostered. Expatriate Europeans have introduced a few golf-courses into the main towns, but not many of them can claim to be of a good standard. Often the greens are "browns"—compacted oil-soaked sand, which is scraped level before putting. A few Batswana have now taken to this game and play it very well.

A more traditional and less active game is played with stones on a "board" marked out in the sand. Groups of men may be seen sitting on the ground playing this.

Mining

The discovery of diamonds brought about a revolutionary change in Botswana. But there are other minerals which are of importance, too. It is diamonds which led to mining now being the largest export industry in the land.

Botswana was the site of the first gold discovered in modern Africa, yet when those mines were worked, other, older shafts were found which remained from centuries before. There have been enough geological and archeological signs to spur on prospectors, striving and hoping for rich discoveries in Botswana, in spite of very trying climatic conditions and very difficult transport problems. In 1955, the big South African mining company, De Beers, obtained concessions to prospect in the Ngwato country. Not until 1967 did they make the tremendous discovery at Orapa, some 240 kilometres (150 miles) west of Francistown. They then formed a company together with the Botswana Government. Initially, Botswana received a minority share of the profits but, following further discoveries, the profits are now equally divided. Orapa started marketing its treasures in 1971. Soon after the discovery of the Orapa pipe, another was found at Lethlakane, just 40 kilometres (25 miles) away. Yet another was discovered in Jwaneng, about 100 kilometres (60 miles) west of Gaborone. This meant that, of six

The Orapa diamond mine, one of three significant diamond pipes discovered in Botswana in the space of just ten years

significant diamond pipes discovered in Africa within a period of ten years, three were in Botswana—the new, poor undeveloped country.

Diamonds are of two main types: gems (precious stones) and industrial diamonds. Usually less than twenty per cent are of gem quality. Diamonds are the hardest substance known to man, and therefore the non-gems are used in drills. Jwaneng is the largest producer of gem diamonds in the world. The addition of the treasures of Jwaneng to those of Orapa and Lethlakane means that Botswana should soon rank as the third largest diamond producer in the world, after Zaire and the USSR. At present Zaire produces fifteen million carats (mainly industrial stones) per annum and the Soviet Union's annual production

51

is twelve million. By 1985 Botswana expects to be producing eleven million carats. The "carat" is a measurement of the weight of a diamond. One carat equals one-fifth of a gram. So that 10,000,000 carats equal two tonnes (and tons are virtually the same).

It is not only the diamonds themselves that are of great value to Botswana. Communications have been needed by the mining industry, so that roads, power and water have been supplied to the mine sites. New towns have been built and this has all created a wide range of job opportunity for Batswana. Orapa

Proving diamonds at Jwaneng. Botswana should soon rank as the third largest diamond producer in the world

and Jwaneng are modern, well laid out towns with housing, schools, medical facilities and leisure activities. There are good living conditions for all who work there.

It will be interesting to see what effect the development of these mining industries in Botswana itself, together with the racial situation in South Africa, will have on the numbers of Batswana men who have left their homes to work in the mines in South Africa. In some ways this "migration" seems almost to have become a kind of replacement for traditional initiation ceremonies—a symbol of coming of age for many young Batswana. For thousands each year, the expected thing to do on reaching manhood was to go to earn money in South African mines—money to save and bring back to the family.

It is, however, a determined policy that eventually Batswana will completely take over all aspects of the work at the mines in Botswana, and the mining company has training programmes aimed at achieving this.

The copper and nickel finds, especially at Selebi-Phikwe, at the end of the 1960s, also caused great excitement. At the beginning of the 1970s this industry was Botswana's greatest investment.

Selebi lies about 50 kilometres (30 miles) east of the railway line, south-east of Francistown. Phikwe is very close by. As a result, the mining town has grown up with the joint name, Selebi-Phikwe. One of the earliest tarred roads in the country was built out to Selebi-Phikwe, and it was linked by rail from the main north-south line. A power-station was constructed here with transmission to Francistown. A huge dam, at Shashe, just west of the railway line, was also built. It is 85 kilometres (about 55 miles) away from the mine, but a pipeline supplies water to serve the mining project.

Unfortunately, trade in copper/nickel exports has not lived up to initial high hopes. In fact, there have been policies to inject other light industries into the town, to make use of the facilities provided and prevent it from becoming a "ghost-town". However, the facts that Shashe Dam is now connected to supply water directly to Francistown and that electricity is similarly supplied to this booming "capital of the north" (Botswana's second town) are possibly sufficient compensation. But Selebi-Phikwe should not be written off. It has a yearly production of nearly 50,000 tonnes of matte, the raw material, which is transported to the USA for further processing.

However promising any industry may be, it is obviously best for a country not to have "all its eggs in one basket". Consequently, it is very encouraging for Botswana that there are large deposits of good quality coal in central Botswana. The reserves are estimated to be very great—around 5,000 million tonnes. There is a colliery at Morupule, west of Palapye, on the road to Serowe. It opened in 1973 and has already been used to supply the power-station at Selebi-Phikwe. But the country's own consumption is, so far, only a tiny fraction of the supplies available. The success of this industry will therefore depend on export trade, which in turn will depend on transportation. Alternatively, coal-generated electricity may be exported to neighbouring countries. At the present time this is hampered by the political problems in southern Africa.

Several other industries may develop to be of even greater value and importance. To the north-west of Francistown is a huge, shallow depression, known as Makgadikgadi Pan. Some think that it may once have been a lake as impressive as Lake Victoria, in Tanzania. But nowadays it is either covered with only an extremely shallow depth of water, or its surface is dry. From the brine deposits of this pan, salt and soda-ash can be obtained. A promising start in obtaining soda ash was made at Sua Pan, a branch of the Makgadikgadi Pan. Although this is closer to the railway, it had to be abandoned because of transportation difficulties. A new attempt is being made to revive this project, which has tremendous potential. At present,

The Makgadikgadi Salt Pan, to the north-west of Francistown

however, there is no world-wide shortage of this material and competitors can sell cheaply.

In the south, not far from Kanye, small quantities of asbestos are quarried. Similarly, there is talc to be obtained in this region; to be used, amongst other things, for making talcum powder. Many other minerals are recorded but their current development varies and is of no great significance. They include gold, silver, kyanite, kaolin, antimony, iron, lead, marble, feldspar, zinc, silica sand, manganese, limestone and uranium. The latter, of course, could be of tremendous importance financially and politically, if it were discovered under the widespread areas of deep Kalahari sand. A few decades ago, geological surveys of such areas were an overwhelming task. But, today, modern techniques—especially using satellite technology—have opened up amazing new possibilities.

One place where you can literally walk along and pick up *semi*-precious stones is Bobonong, which is about 120 kilometres (75 miles) east of the railway, out past Selebi-Phikwe. Officially, one has to obtain permission to gather them; but there are many little boys who will offer agate, tiger-eyes, jasper and many other stones, for a few coins.

A Tour of Botswana

We will be travelling by car and will be on tarred roads almost all the way, something which would have been impossible before about 1983. Ten years before that, of the 8,000 kilometres (5,000 miles) of roads in the country only about 64 kilometres (40 miles) were asphalted. What we shall see is the newly developed Botswana. But not many visitors get out into the real wilds; and many foreigners, and even Batswana, only see a very small fraction of the country.

Our journey will begin at Lobatse in the far south-east. This is close to the new South African homeland of Bophuthatswana, and many visitors enter the country by this route, either by car or train. This was Bechuanaland's second largest town. Now it is a pleasant little place which does not look as important as it really is. Its influence lies more in the fact that it is the focal point of a large farming area. It is here that the Botswana Meat Commission has its impressive organization. The High Court of Botswana is also situated in Lobatse. Between 1960 and 1965, before Gaborone became the new capital, the legislative council met in a courthouse just north of the town.

Off our route to the north-west is Kanye, one of the largest villages in the land. It is the tribal capital of the Bangwaketse. From Kanye the desert road continues its long, hot, dusty way

57

A bus station in Francistown. Although travel by bus has increased tremendously since more main roads have been tarred, many of the vehicles used are quite old

to Ghanzi, right over near Namibia on the far western side of Botswana. On the way we would pass the turn-off to Jwaneng, the latest diamond mine.

The drive to Gaborone is along one of the most scenically attractive parts of the route, as the countryside is comparatively hilly. Otherwise, Botswana's high ground is confined to small hills which are outcrops of rock, called *kopje*. We now pass close to Ramotswa. This is the capital of the Balete, and has a population of about 20,000 in a rather compact village.

Gaborone has grown rapidly, from a very small beginning.

58

It is the capital and the seat of the government, which meets in the National Assembly building. Gaborone is on the Ngotwane River, very close to the border with South Africa.

Being virtually a new town, it has been planned for further growth. But when it reached 40,000 inhabitants in 1979, few would have anticipated a population of more than 130,000, which is now expected by 1990. Certainly, those who planned the dam which supplies the town's water did not anticipate such growth. The level of the dam has been dangerously low in the recent droughts.

The residence of the president, most governmental departments and the head offices of business organizations are all located here. A large industrial area and railway yard have grown since the original construction of the capital. The centre of Gaborone is the pedestrian shopping mall, which was such

The Botswana National Assembly building in Gaborone. The government meets here

a unique phenomenon in the country in the early 1970s. But more and more housing (as well as shanty dwellings) results in an ever-spreading capital, as people are attracted to work here. Urbanization and associated crime are serious problems for the authorities to deal with.

As we leave the capital we pass a road leading to Molepolole, the third largest of the traditional villages. Its administrative district is very large and sparsely populated. The first new training college for teachers in junior secondary schools is situated here.

Almost on the main road north and only a little way out of

A pictorial tapestry made at Oodi near Gaborone. These tapestries, sold worldwide, depict traditional scenes and stories

Gaborone is the little settlement of Oodi. Here a group of weavers, under the initial guidance of some Danes, has established a fine reputation for its pictorial tapestries which are now sold world-wide. They mainly show traditional scenes and tell stories of the country, past and present. There are no standard patterns, as each weaver is a creative artist.

Back on the main road once more, we soon come to another turning which we should not just rush by. We are just north of Gaborone. This road to the east leads to Mochudi, just a few minutes' drive from the main road. It is the capital of the Bakgatla. It is attractively situated in a hilly area with the traditional setting around the main *kgotla*. The oldest secondary school in the country is here. It has now been converted into a museum.

As we rejoin the main road at Pilane, we may be tempted to stop and admire the many examples of leathercraft which are a speciality here.

But we have a long journey still ahead of us and many places to visit. We can now cover quite a long distance to our next stopping-place, Mahalapye. Just before we get there we may see a road-side sign TROPIC OF CAPRICORN. It is interesting to pull off the road for a few minutes, as we enter the tropics, to see an instrument set up to mark the spot. If we are fortunate enough to time our visit to be at noon on December 21st, we will see that the sun, being exactly overhead, shines vertically down the mounted tube.

Mahalapye is on the railway line which we have been

A view of Mochudi, the capital of the Bakgatla

following very closely all the way north. Even in developing Botswana, petrol filling stations are few and far between, so that it is a good idea to fill up here, about half way to Francistown from Gaborone. Mahalapye is growing slowly, but is mainly a farming centre. Not far away the remains of the London Missionary School, from the 1860s, are still to be seen. A road also leads to the Shoshong Hills, a previous capital of the Bamangwato.

Continuing north, we come to Palapye, an important railway siding. The place has grown in importance since Serowe became the capital of the Bamangwato. If we make a detour to the east, before continuing to Francistown, we shall soon pass the Morupule Colliery, and then we come to Serowe.

62

Serowe is Botswana's historic village and a large, traditional one. Here the main attraction for tourists is the burial hill of the Khama family, where the grave of Khama III may be seen, surmounted by the bronze figure of a small antelope called a duiker. This is the totem of the tribe.

Serowe has one of Botswana's four teacher training colleges for primary teachers. Unlike the others, it is for women only. Serowe is also the home of the Brigades movement which began in 1965, being introduced by Patrick van Rensburg. The Brigades were basically an attempt to provide further education, largely of a practical nature, for those not able to get a place in a secondary school. The idea was to provide a kind of

This instrument is situated by the side of the road between Gaborone and Francistown. It marks the latitude of the Tropic of Capricorn and is a popular stopping-place for tourists

THIS POINT IS ON THE TROPIC OF CAPRICORN, WHICH IS THE MOST SOUTHERLY LATITUDE REACHED BY THE SUN. HERE THE SUN WILL BE AT THE ZENITH EACH YEAR ON MIDSUMMER DAY AT MIDDAY LOCAL APPARENT TIME WHICH IS ON 22 DECEMBER AT APPROXIMATELY 13 MINUTES PAST TWELVE O' CLOCK NOON. AT THE ABOVE TIME THE SUN WILL SHINE DIRECTLY DOWN THE TUBE ABOVE THIS NOTICE.

Serowe—an historic village for the Batswana. The burial hill of the Khama family—including the grave of Khama III—is situated here

apprenticeship in skills such as building, motor mechanics, electrical skills, tanning, carpentry and textiles.

Our next junction on the road north is at Serule. From here we could drive east to Selebi-Phikwe and the copper and nickel mines. If we were attracted by the thought of picking up semi-precious stones, we could continue, but on a dirt road, to Bobonong.

Still following the railway very closely, we are taken past the large, quite attractive village of Tonota, before we cross the Shashe River, which is almost certain to be just a bed of sand, as it is for all except just a few weeks of the year.

Shashe villagers specialize in making and selling wood-carvings in hard reddish-brown mophane wood. They swarm along the platform when the daily passenger train comes in, offering their wares. Some sit by the road-side, hoping to attract motorists. Also at the side of the road, just before the bridge, is a *rondavel* bearing the sign Botswanacraft. It is the sales-room of a company devoted to the development and marketing of Botswana's handcrafts. The speciality in Botswana is probably the attractively designed baskets, decorated with many different patterns. There are also wood-carvings, traditional stools, traditional musical instruments and, always popular, Bushman articles and Herero dolls.

But not many motorists slow down here unless they are prepared to turn off to visit Shashe Dam, over a rough but fairly short road which leads to the huge, artificial lake. Here there are plenty of aquatic birds and waders, even some pelicans.

Francistown is 30 kilometres (18 miles) away; and that is about the distance that the town's water supply is now pumped. As the town grew, reliance on its nine boreholes became less certain. Francistown is now the envy of Gaborone as far as this long-lasting supply of water is concerned.

Francistown is an important railway centre. Botswana hopes to take over responsibility for the section of the line which passes through its territory, and the headquarters of Botswana Railways will be in Francistown. Large quantities of cattle are loaded here for transportation south to the abattoir in Lobatse. Francistown is almost the only place in Botswana which does not have a Setswana name. The town is named after Daniel Francis, who was a prospector and miner here in the second half of the nineteenth century.

These baskets of palm leaf are decorated with traditional motifs and are given names such as "face of the zebra", "tears of the giraffe" and "knees of the tortoise"

Few people come to Francistown for its own sake. Those travelling north are usually on their way to visit game parks and similar holiday attractions.

Francistown has changed in recent years and developed at an amazing rate. Shops are increasing in number and improving in appearance. There is also a pedestrian shopping mall with supermarkets. The disproportionately large number of clothing shops is a rather sad indication of the amount of increased income which is now being spent in Botswana on clothes—a status symbol. Recently, a very fine, well-appointed cinema has added to the almost incredible changes. An attractive park has been achieved where just a few years ago there was "bush".

66

Two modern, attractive hotels have sprung up. And the previously small industrial site grows rapidly.

The second main airport of Botswana is situated in Francistown, although the present airport facilities for passengers are rather incongruous compared with the size of aircraft which could land on its extended runway. But it copes adequately with the 50-seater planes which currently use the airport on their regular routes, with just two or three landings a day.

Our Tour Continues

Travellers passing through Francistown by road have a choice of three routes. If they continue more or less due north they will still be following the railway and will enjoy a good, new tarred road which, in 1983, replaced the bone-jarring, car-damaging, poor dirt road to the border with Zimbabwe, at Ramokgwebane. At this place the railway will have completed 630 kilometres (394 miles) within the country, on its run north. From that point it is just 7 kilometres (4 miles) of dirt road, in no-man's land, so to speak, before the Zimbabwe border town of Plumtree and then 100 kilometres (60 miles) of good, tarred road, through Matabeleland to Bulawayo, the second city of Zimbabwe.

It is an interesting sign of the times that only a few years ago, people drove from Francistown to Bulawayo, in spite of the road, to do extra shopping there. Now it is the other way round, and there is a good road to help the traffic.

Another road out of Francistown runs almost due west to the diamond-mining town of Orapa. It is a three-hour bumpy ride still to reach this very security-conscious town. But there will doubtless be a good road before many more years.

The road that will be our route out of Francistown heads north-west, past the Orapa turn-off. We will have to stop at

68

Dukwe where there is a cordon fence, in connection with controls against foot-and-mouth disease, though it is no longer necessary for the wheels of vehicles and the shoes of passengers to be sprayed. Dukwe is also the site of a large refugee camp, housing those who have fled from neighbouring countries.

Further on, we have the chance to turn off along a rough track. This leads to Sua Pan and the site of the soda-ash project. It also provides a view of the seemingly endless salt-flats, most probably shimmering with a mirage. Even when apparently dry, with a parched, cracked surface, this area is treacherously misleading and motorists who venture on it in an ordinary vehicle are very likely to stick fast. Here we may be fortunate enough to see thousands upon thousands of flamingoes, though probably a long way off. In flight, some of their flocks have been calculated to extend to as much as 16 kilometres (10 miles). We may, of course, only find a single pink feather lying on the pan. Perhaps, as a compensation, we may see the very attractive bat-eared fox who cautiously approaches through the grass on the edges of the pan.

Once north of Sua Pan, back on the main road, we start to notice a change in the scenery. To be honest, our drive from Gaborone, so far, has offered little of scenic beauty or much which could be called attractive. But here, at least, there is a change. We are at the nearest point to the desert. Just south of the village of Nata we begin to see palm trees, and a few baobab trees, which have been aptly described as ''upside-down trees''. They have a somewhat pinkish, fairly soft covering.

Many parts of these trees can be used for different purposes; they are the source of drinks, cups and vessels, soap, shampoo, paper, medicine, soup, vegetable, glue, cream of tartar . . . and even sometimes shelter for a bus-load of passengers. There is one near Kasane which was once used as a jail. Just south of Nata is a likely place to see ostriches, probably speeding along over open ground.

Nata is a pleasant little village at which to stop, before facing another choice of route. It is on the Nata River which flows from Zimbabwe into the Makgadikgadi Pan. Nata has grown in population at an alarming rate. Quite literally, alarming, because of the water problems there. There is very little ground water and what there is, is very salty. Yet, strangely, the growth in population is largely due to the fact that people have flocked there from places that are even drier. Each day a water-carrying bowser delivers supplies from 40 kilometres (25 miles) away.

Now we turn almost due west and skirt along the north of the Makgadikgadi Pan, heading for Maun. This is still a dirt road, though a fairly good one, apart from during the rainy season. It is already in the first stages of becoming a tarred road. When it is, it will make a tremendous difference to Maun.

Since 1983, the other choice of road out of Nata, more or less due north, has been tarred, and that now provides a smooth ride to Kasane and the Kazungula ferry to Zambia, across the Zambesi. This is still a very small and crude affair. At Kasane there are the approaches to the Chobe Game Park but there is little of interest along this lengthy stretch of road, unless an

Lake Ngami, an excellent place for bird-watching

elephant should suddenly lumber across it further to the north.

But we are on the other road, heading towards Maun. About half way along there is a turn-off to the north, to Nxai Pan National Park (Nxai is pronounced with a click of the tongue). This is one of the less-publicized game parks, but it is claimed that here it is possible to see thousands of head of wildebeest (gnu) and zebra in a day. The pan is a fossil lake-bed which must at one time have been linked to the larger Makgadikgadi Pan.

But our journey carries us on to Maun. Maun is the centre from which visitors set out to the Okavango Delta and the Moremi Wildlife Reserve, although the village is still unattractive in itself. It is the administrative capital of the Batawana and Ngamiland.

The road continues to Lake Ngami which is a fine place for

71

bird-watching, when there is water. It is also a sickeningly sad place full of the carcases of cattle and wildlife when there is not enough water. Having passed Lake Ngami, the road goes on all the way to Ghanzi, in the far west, but the going is rough.

The Tsodilo Hills with its Bushmen and well-known rock-paintings is another difficult drive from Maun, across some very inhospitable terrain away to the far north-west. Most visitors fly in.

It is mainly the unique Okavango Delta which attracts people to Maun. Although the source of the Okavango, which is the third largest river in southern Africa, rises in Angola (no very great distance from the Atlantic Ocean to the west), it flows east and south into the delta, where at flood time it spreads out over an area of almost 15,000 square kilometres (6,000 square miles) of meandering waterways, flooded plains and lagoons or islands

An aerial view of the Boro River in the Okavango Delta, the greatest inland delta in the world

of palms. These floods (in May to August) do not coincide with the rains in Botswana, but depend on the flooded river higher in Angola.

Only a very small fraction of the water passes through the swamps, and this either drains into Lake Ngami or eventually just disappears into the Kalahari Desert. The Boteti River leads the waters towards the Makgadikgadi Pan.

The delta is mainly uninhabited except for scattered groups of River Bushmen. The means of transport on the waters is a dug-out canoe, called a *mekoro*, which is carried over the dividing land between.

This, the greatest inland delta in the world, created by shifts in the earth's surface, is an intriguing area. There are numerous sites for visitors, ranging from the primitive to the luxurious; close to Maun itself or deep in the heart of the delta. There is something for all who are interested in wildlife: game, fish, birds, plant-life and numerous crocodiles in the myriad waterways.

Within the delta area is the Moremi Wildlife Reserve—in all probability one of the most spectacular and beautiful game reserves to be found in southern Africa. It was created by the Batswana on their land, in 1962, and is preserved by restricting tourist facilities and keeping the area as natural as possible.

If we are to leave this fascinating region and continue our journey without doubling back on our tracks, we will need a four-wheel-drive vehicle to enable us to drive through the Chobe National Park and reach Kasane and the Kazungula ferry.

Chobe is regarded by those fortunate enough to have been

Travelling in a *mekoro*, or dug-out canoe — the main means of transport in the Okavango Delta

there as one of the finest game parks in the world. It is situated on the Chobe River, the country's natural border to the north. Within its area there is said to be the largest concentration and variety of game in Africa. It is particularly noted for huge herds of elephants, numbered at 30,000, which cause extensive devastation to the trees and shrubs. It is necessary to cull elephants regularly, in an attempt to keep numbers under control. Game-viewing is easiest in the dry season (May to September), when the game come down to the river for water.

On this journey we have learned about some marvellous areas for viewing game but it did not take us near to the Kalahari Gemsbok National Park, which is an even larger remote wildlife reserve. It stretches over the south-west corner of Botswana and extends into South Africa. It is the home of great herds of gemsbok (oryx) and other antelope species. And, as well as other

74

members of the large cat-family, it is famous for the black-maned lion.

In addition, in the centre of Botswana is the Khutse and Central Kalahari Game Reserve, almost as extensive as all the others put together. Here there are huge herds of migratory springbok, zebra and wildebeest. It is also the main hunting-ground of one of the world's most primitive people, the Kalahari Bushmen.

As we continue, we leave the western end of Chobe and approach Kasane and Kazungula. We have come to the northernmost point of our journey, and its end. From here, visitors may leave Botswana across the Zambesi into Zambia or probably visit the mighty Victoria Falls, just one hour's drive

Elephants at a waterhole in Chobe National Park

Impala, a type of antelope. These graceful animals can frequently be seen in Chobe National Park

away in Zimbabwe. The potential for tourism in Botswana is enormous, but much which is priceless may be lost in the process of development. The authorities are well aware of this and strive to protect the wildlife areas which are rapidly becoming almost unique in Africa.

Transport, Communications, Education and Health

Probably the greatest developments in Botswana in modern times have been in transport and communications. This is most obvious in the explosive growth and improvement in roads. A tremendous amount of foreign aid money has helped to bring about the transformation. The number of cars is increasing rapidly, but still the donkey-cart is the means of transport for thousands.

Air transport is beginning to improve and Botswana plans to take over the running of the railway within its borders.

Although the number of cars in Botswana is increasing rapidly, donkey-carts such as this one are still the main means of transport for thousands of people

Growing industry will desperately need improved transport facilities. The single-line track with loops at numerous little sidings is not going to be an adequate railway system for the future.

Telecommunications have also improved immensely in recent years. A satellite-earth station at Gaborone, and other technological improvements, now enable Botswana to be independent of the systems belonging to neighbouring countries. Telephone, telex, and telegraph services are in operation. But the postal service still has difficulties in reaching remote areas without delays. The country still does not have its own television service, but it is possible to receive programmes from South

Francistown railway station. Botswana is soon to take over the running of its own railway system from Zimbabwe Railways

Crowded classrooms and lack of suitable accommodation result in many classes being held out of doors, as in this photograph

Africa. Botswana Radio, however, is well established and also includes broadcasts for schools.

The basis on which future independent development must be built is education. Schooling is not compulsory in Botswana but has recently become free, at primary (elementary) level. Most children do now attend school, and many schools are very overcrowded. Very many classes have no classroom and pupils take it in turns for their class to spend a week out-of-doors, under the shade of a tree. For most of the year, the climate does not make this too unbearable. Conditions are still very primitive in far too many schools, with no chairs and/or desks even for the classrooms. It is difficult to find enough teachers with

79

sufficient education themselves to be able to teach others. The four teacher training colleges provide about seven hundred qualified teachers annually. Many of these are not new young entrants to the profession but unqualified teachers who are now trained.

Secondary schools are usually boarding-schools and there are not enough places available for the increasing numbers of children finishing their primary education. This has resulted in the growth of private secondary schools as well as the State ones.

The University of Botswana is in Gaborone and is doing its best to provide the kind of educated manpower that the country will so desperately need to achieve localization. Many students still get their higher education in a variety of countries outside Botswana, either before or after attending Botswana's own university.

The health of the nation must not be overlooked. Tuberculosis is widespread and it will probably be a long time before it is kept in check. Bilharzia and sleeping sickness are serious diseases which are being fought with growing success. Malaria which is not widespread, being mainly confined to the wetter north-west swamp areas, is now far less of a problem with the availability of modern medicine.

The Batawana have a great fear of snakes. There are more than fifty different species in the country and about ten of these are very poisonous. These include cobras, mambas and the

The Bushmen

The Tsodilo Hills, to the north-wast of Maun, are referred to as the home of the Kalahari Bushmen. But Bushmen are spread over a much wider area and it is estimated that about 50,000 live in Botswana and Namibia, with some spreading into Zimbabwe and Angola. They are called Basarwa in Setswana and the official name for these primitive people is the San.

Little is known for certain about their origins, but they have been extensively studied and popularized in more recent decades. But probably there are not as many as five per cent of Bushmen who nowadays live in the traditional way of life that has been photographed, filmed and written about so much recently. Anthropologists have been keen to record the life of this fast-disappearing traditional life-style as integration into another way of living, and with other tribes, becomes inevitable.

There are three main features which characterize the appearance of the Bushmen. They are rather short, their skin is a light golden brown and the women, in particular, tend to accumulate fat around the buttocks. Many Bushmen mingle with members of more settled communities and often work on cattle-posts. But they have a tendency to be restless and to disappear for some months, back to the life of freedom, as lived by their forefathers for many generations. For this reason they are often regarded as unreliable.

It is interesting, in a part of the world which is so concerned with racial discrimination, that the Batswana tend to look down on the Bushmen. As other Batswana spread their farms and cattle-ranches into the areas where the Bushman had hunted for centuries, he found it easier, or necessary, to steal cattle—which obviously gained him a bad reputation.

The primitive Bushmen are probably best known for their ability to survive in this extremely arid area, by hunting and somehow managing to obtain liquid. Their rock paintings are also world-famous. Traditionally, they are nomads and they wander in groups varying between less than ten, up to thirty or more. Their temporary homes are made by simply leaning a few small branches together, to provide some shade from the heat of the sun and a little protection from cool night winds. They scrape a hollow in which to sleep and have acquired the habit of sleeping in a posture which raises their heads from the ground, presumably to reduce the nuisance of crawling insects. They are always alert to the danger of prowling lions. They wear little clothing; usually nothing more than a loin-cloth—just a minimal piece of animal skin which is tied with a strip of leather. As decoration they may wear beads, often made from the shells of ostrich eggs and smaller birds. Some may wear an animal skin slung around the shoulders, like a shawl.

A very large part of their food is gathered—mainly by the women. Different types of wild melons are collected, as are

84

so-called monkey-oranges. They pick wild berries, collect birds' eggs and sometimes honey. They also catch lizards, insects and snakes for food. They have no obvious source of water, apart from the widely scattered boreholes, but they manage to obtain liquid and survive. Over many centuries they have learned to follow the signs which tell them where water may lie beneath the parched surface, or where bulbous roots containing moisture may be grubbed out and squeezed to extract precious liquid. They use the long hollow stem of a plant as a drinking-straw. They push it down through the sand and suck up water, storing it in their mouths, to be emptied into hollow gourds which serve as containers. Sometimes water may be stored in the very large shells of ostrich eggs buried in the sand for future use. The egg shells are sealed with a grass plug and sometimes they are marked with a symbol, for identification.

The men are accomplished hunters and remarkable trackers; their survival depends on their ability. They tip their hunting arrows with a deadly poison, carefully extracted from the pupae of two special beetles. This poison has the effect of slowly paralyzing their victim; but, before it is finally too weak to escape, they may have to follow it for a long way. They also use snares, many of which are partly string, made from a plant similar to sisal.

The food they obtain is shared equally amongst the whole group. To make a fire for cooking they must create a spark by rubbing two dry sticks together; one held between the feet and the other twirled rapidly between the palms of their hands. Once

A Bushman hunter. The Bushmen are well known for their ability as hunters and trackers

kindled, the fire is carefully preserved and controlled. A roaring blaze is usually not needed, except perhaps for protection against predators at night. To avoid wasting precious supplies of scarce wood, a smouldering ash is maintained.

The Bushmen are great story-tellers. They all gather round to hear tales told by the older members of the group, about past adventures. They are also good mimics and even if one does not understand their unusual language (called Khoison), which is punctuated continuously by various and numerous clicking noises made with the tongue against the inside of the mouth, it is very easy to recognize from their body antics and gesticulations, the animal they are describing when recounting some hunting escapade.

As well as telling stories, the Bushmen dance a lot. This is often part of a deeply religious experience for the Basarwa and leads them into a trance.

The Bushman rock-paintings are several hundreds of years old. Some are estimated at more than a thousand years. Those preseved are often found in caves where they have been protected from the elements. They mainly depict animals; often in a hunting scene. The form is clear and simple, as are the colurs which were made from natural pigments found by the artists. The engravings have been patiently hacked out of the rock with the small points of primitive tools. The Tsodilo Hills are a ridge

Bushman rock-paintings in the Tsodilo Hills

Bushmen outside one of their temporary huts made from leaning a few branches together

of rocky outcrops nearly 20 kilometres (12 miles) long, and there are more than two thousand rock paintings in this area. But the Bushman paintings are survivals of an age-old traditional art which has mysteriously died out. There are no Bushman artists nowadays.

Unfortunately, one cannot think about the Bushmen without a certain amount of sadness. In striving after so many of the "better" things which development brings, there are dangers that they will be losing priceless advantages which have been lost to so-called civilized cultures, often irreplacably.

This is true, not only for the Bushmen, but for Botswana as a whole. Progress is galloping on. Nothing will prevent it.

Through Independence into the Future

When Sir Seretse Khama became Botswana's first president, in 1966, he recognized the need for strong leadership. Whilst he grew to be even more accepted as a wise leader within his own country, his realistic diplomacy was respected by the majority of countries throughout the world. He always regarded himself as the representative of his government, party and people and was in no way dictatorial.

The form of constitution created by the new leaders was a very clever mixture of some of the best aspects of American and British types of democracy. It combined a presidential power, as in the USA, with a strong legislature, as in Britain. Since independence, local government in Botswana has been divided into twelve councils. Nine of these are districts and the other three are Gaborone, Lobatse and Francistown. In addition to their local responsibilities, they may raise taxes from residents in their areas.

Another wise move was to incorporate a House of Chiefs, to advise the government on main issues, although there is no debate and the government is not bound to heed the advice given. Incidentally, Botswana is one of the few countries in Africa which has a multi-party system, with opposition parties.

Troubles in neighbouring Rhodesia, on its way to becoming

independent Zimbabwe, and refugees from South Africa, together with pressures from African countries further away from the "front-line", required all the diplomatic ability that Sir Seretse Khama, and his advisers, possessed.

The next general election was in 1969. The percentage of registered voters who turned up to the polls to vote was reduced, this time by a third. Some say that it was political apathy in Botswana, others say that the people had already made their choice and could not understand why they had to repeat themselves. They were used to having a chief for his lifetime. Others interpreted it as being an expression of satisfaction with the government, since people felt confident that it would be re-elected without their vote. Whatever the reasons, the Botswana Democratic Party has remained in power with only a slight increase in the representation of other parties.

But news of Sir Seretse Khama's serious ill-health was becoming more widely known. People were beginning to wonder if Botswana's initial successful start as an independent country would be maintained under other leadership. There had been the sort of disaster in other African countries, followed by extreme political unrest.

Sir Seretse died on July 13th, 1980, at the age of fifty-nine. He was sincerely mourned by the vast majority of his people and sorely missed by many statesmen outside Botswana's borders.

He was quickly succeeded, on July 18th, 1980, by Dr. Quett Masire, who had been the vice-president and secretary general of the Botswana Democratic Party. Sir Seretse's selection of a member of the Bangwaketse as successor was, perhaps, another example of uniting the tribes into the nation. In one of his early speeches, the new president said, ''It is the policies which the late president has been following which I, together with my colleagues in the government, intend to follow.''

In many countries a change of leadership is accompanied by the immediate removal of all signs of the old regime. But in Botswana, it was a long time before pictures of the new president appeared in official buildings. Even then, they appeared alongside that of Sir Seretse. Similarly, new bank-notes bearing a likeness of Dr. Masire, did not appear for a considerable time.

This unassuming new president slowly gained the confidence and respect of the people, as a worthy replacement of the first president of Botswana, who had had the great Khama lineage behind him.

The 1984 general election was the first since Quett Masire had become president. There are now thirty-four constituencies. There appeared to be more interest in political issues this time. The ruling Botswana Democratic Party won twenty-nine seats, with the Botswana National Front winning four and the Botswana People's Party just one. Thus BDP maintains its political domination and the present government is generally popular.

So, President Masire and Botswana go forward into the unknown Future. Much has been achieved in a short space of time. The country is trying to catch up in a few decades what has taken centuries elsewhere. A poor country, Botswana is even beginning to show signs of prosperity in a few areas; development is going ahead at a remarkable rate, tightropes in politics have been successfully negotiated and internal government has been stable.

There is, however, a tendency for the rich to become richer whilst the poor stay poor. Will this lead to eventual discontent which will be exploited and aggravated by political interests outside the country? What effect will changes in neighbouring countries have on Botswana, which has such a good record of racial integration and harmony? Only the future will tell.

The Botswana coat of arms. The word *Pula* means "Let there be rain" and is used both as a greeting and as a farewell

Index

94